THE

DUTY OF THE HOUR.

BY

REV. SAMUEL T. SPEAR, D.D.,

PASTOR OF THE SOUTH PRESBYTERIAN CHURCH OF BROOKLYN.

NEW-YORK:
ANSON D. F. RANDOLPH, 683 BROADWAY.

1863.

THE DUTY OF THE HOUR.

Esther 4 : 14.

"And who knoweth whether thou art come to the kingdom for such a time as this?"

These words were addressed by Mordecai to Esther, the wife of Ahasuerus, the Persian monarch. Esther was by birth a Jewess, by condition a captive, by marriage a queen, by her mission the elect of Providence to save her people from destruction. An awful crisis had arrived in the history of the Jews; by a royal decree they were doomed to general extermination; and Mordecai, wishing to secure her interposition in their behalf, suggests that perhaps she had "come to the kingdom for such a time as this." Constrained by the argument, she gave herself to the service, and was the means of saving her people. Great crises in human affairs often, yea generally, either create or find the agency suited to their demands.

Thus, on the twenty-second day of February, in the year 1732, just one hundred and thirty-one years ago to-day, was born a man whom God gave to the world, and especially to this country, as one of the richest legacies of his Providence. He was forty-four years of age when our forefathers proclaimed their independence of the British Crown. He was chosen as the commander-in-chief of the army during that memorable struggle which finally ended in victory, and made us a free and independent people. He was twice elected to the Presidency of the United States. Having served his country in the field, and in the highest civil station known to the laws of this land, he died on the fourteenth of December, 1799, in the sixty-seventh year of his age. He was a patriot and a Christian, a great and good man, heroic on the battle-field and wise as a statesman. We speak of him as the Father of our country. The American people have been accustomed to hail the anniversary of his birthday, which this year falls on the Sabbath, with special marks of respect to his memory. I need not say to you that George Washington is the person of whom I am speaking. In his age he was the man for the times. In the midst of great difficulties, in the face of severe opposition, often assailed by party jealousy, sometimes almost supplanted in his position, always resisted by the Tories, he nevertheless held firmly to his course, and guided the Revolutionary struggle to victory and success. Humanly speaking, the effort must have failed without Washington. Just as he was completing his last term of Presidential service, he issued his "Farewell Address" to the American people, warning them against the spirit of party, and urging upon them the great importance of the Union for their common prosperity.

Having nobly done his work, alike as the soldier and the statesman, Washington has been sleeping in his grave for more than half a century.

The country to whose good he devoted his life, has advanced in all the elements of national greatness. The Constitution and the Government which he helped to frame, have until recently been the watchwords, the glory and pride of all the people. The Union has proved its wisdom by its great blessings. We have rejoiced in it, and supposed it to be permanent.

Where are we now? What is the present state of our country? It is a little more than two years since South-Carolina began the work of secession. She was soon followed by other States. Soon these seceding States were organized into a Confederate Government; and soon thereafter the nation's flag was assailed at Fort Sumter. War then commenced—a civil war—a war between the Government of the United States and a portion of its rebellious citizens—a war on the part of the Government to preserve the Union, and on the part of the rebels to destroy it—a war for which the loyal people were almost wholly unprepared—a war that has swollen into vast dimensions—I may add, a war which, though not always decisive in particular combats, and certainly not yet ended, has been one of very decided progress to the Federal arms, securing on the side of the Government great advantages, and giving good promise of final victory.

In the commencement, which was the moment of patriotic passion rather than of mature and long-sighted reflection, there seemed to be a very great unanimity of opinion and feeling among the Northern people in respect to this war. Public sentiment was so near a unit that the exceptions were comparatively rare. The language of sympathy with treason was not heard on many lips; and, when heard, provoked the contempt which it always deserves. Newspapers that had hitherto shown strong tendencies to favor the secessionists, were suddenly converted to the doctrines of loyalty. The truth is, the war was popular, so much so, that it swept all opposition before it.

Since that period, and during the progress of the struggle, various causes have arisen to agitate and disturb the public mind, to set men to thinking, and to call out diversities and conflicts of opinion. The same things existed in the war of the Revolution, and in that of 1812; and they are likely to exist in any war conducted by a free people. They can be avoided only by an absolute despotism, that crushes freedom of thought and freedom of speech. War is a tremendously exciting business; it presents a vast many questions; and hence it need be no matter of surprise if the people do not all see alike. The fact should frighten no one, and stir no man's passions to unreasonable violence.

We have all shared in some degree of *disappointment*, mainly, as I think, because our expectations in the outset were entirely unreasonable. We expected to finish this work with a rush, and in a short time. The popular idea of war is that of speedy victory followed by peace, without any due consideration of what war means, or what are its difficulties; and hence, when this result is not at once gained, the public heart is very likely to yield to "unmanly depression," and vent its passions upon the Government. Under such circumstances we must have something to find fault with; and the most tangible object is the Government. Every man wants to be the Government; and if the result be not what he expected, then, in his judgment, it is because his policy was not adopted.

Some of us, too, have, at times, felt some degree of *despondency* as to the final result; and if we have talked as we have felt, we have communicated this feeling to each other. War, especially such as the one in which we are engaged, tries men's hearts; it tries their power of hope; it tries their patience; and there are some men who are not able to bear this trial. They break down under it. If they are not positive croakers themselves, they are in a very good condition to listen to this mode of talking, and to be seriously affected by it.

There is also among the people an honest *dissatisfaction* with the method in which the Government has conducted this war. The people are not agreed as to the method; and since we are all generals, and would be glad to be Presidents, there must, of course, be some collision here. Some do not like the Proclamation, and others do like it. Some complain of military arrests, and others think them perfectly justifiable. To the eyes of some there is an unusual amount of corruption at Washington, while others of equal capacity, equal candor, and equal opportunities to judge, see no evidence of any such thing. There is no use in ignoring the fact, that honest men, good citizens, persons who mean to be faithful to their country, do not agree as to the method in which this war has been conducted; and the same fact would exist under any policy which it is possible for the Government to adopt. It need surprise nobody; and if we are a reasonable and a true people, it ought not to harm any body. We may make it the source of a tremendous evil; yet I hope better things of the American people.

There is again a class of persons scattered through the loyal States, small as compared with the whole body of the people, of whom one hates to think. They are out-and-out *traitors*, clearly such in *feeling*, and, so far as they dare to be so, such in *practice*. They have no sympathy with the Government in this struggle for life. They rejoice "when the rebels are successful," and are "cast down when victory attends the Federal arms." Some of them are in official positions, and some of them are editors of newspapers. If they were at the South, they would be rebels themselves. They are such in feeling. Their sympathies lie wholly with the enemy. The conduct of such persons is indeed a great trial to the patience of patriotic feeling. It is no slander to call them traitors, since this is their proper title.

In addition to this, we have in the loyal States a somewhat violent display of *party* spirit, instigated and conducted by political leaders, who simply want the places of power, and make the war an occasion for gaining this end. They must, of course, attack the Government. They must denounce its policy. They must do what they can to impair the confidence of the people in our present national rulers. All this is necessary as belonging to the machinery of party tactics. These men, I shall do them the justice to believe, do not actually mean to ruin the country. What they mean, is to place the political power of the country in their own hands. They are partisans when they ought to be patriots.

I have thus set before you some of the causes of the present agitation and conflicts in the public mind. Our present position as a people is a state of war with a very formidable foe, somewhat complicated by these causes. We are not to-day as harmonious in the prosecution of this war as we seemed to be twelve months ago. Such is the plain matter of fact.

Now, looking the facts squarely in the face, I wish to state to you the positive and absolute *necessity* of our position. The enemy with whom we are contending, will make no peace with this Government that is not based on disunion. The evidence on this point is so abundant that I do not see how any one can doubt it. You can not propose any other terms of peace with the rebel authorities at Richmond which they will consider for even a moment. So they explicitly say, and so all their actions prove. I believe this to be a fixed fact. I hence come to the conclusion that the Government must actually crush this rebellion by force of arms, and thus conquer a peace, and in this way preserve the Union, or that we must consent to disunion. This is what I mean by the *necessity* of our position; and let me tell you that I see no possible escape from it. We may regret it; we may deplore the terrible evils of war; we may differ as to the causes of this bloody contest; we may complain of this or that measure of the Government; we may contend among ourselves, and thus divide our strength; but here we are as a whole people, driven right up to this necessity, in a state of war with an armed rebellion which we must conquer, or by which we must be conquered. We must succeed or fail. If we fail, we shall all go down together, Democrats and Republicans, the supporters and the opponents of the war, the politicians and the common people, pro-slavery men and anti-slavery men, saints and sinners. "We shall all be saved together, or all lost together." We are all in this ship of State, and if it founders we shall all founder with it. Those who can not see the hopeless destruction of the Union by the defeat of the Government in this struggle, seem to me strangely infatuated. Those who suppose that their political enemies are to be the only sufferers in the event of such a disaster are greatly mistaken. We are *one* people, living under a common government; and as such we must share together in the common prosperity and glory, or the common disgrace and ruin of our common nationality. In the national sense, we shall die together, or live together.

Having thus stated the case, as I have desired to do, with plainness and candor, I come now to inquire into the great and urgent *duty* of the hour. What *ought* we to do, as a people, in "such a time as this?" The answer which I shall give to this question, and earnestly commend to your consideration, is this: WE OUGHT BY EVERY MEANS IN OUR POWER TO SUSTAIN THE GOVERNMENT OF THESE UNITED STATES IN THE PROSECUTION OF THIS WAR. This I hold to be the cardinal duty of the hour. Let me in a word explain its meaning.

By the Government I mean the agency for which the Constitution has provided, and which the people, acting under this Constitution, have created for the enactment and enforcement of national laws. This is the Government; and of this Government Abraham Lincoln is now the Constitutional Executive. He is also the "Commander-in-Chief" of the Army and Navy. Not long since I saw in one of the New-York papers this phrase: "The Government, *as it is called.*" What did the editor mean by the clause "*as it is called*"? I will not answer the question; yet any man of common-sense will readily detect the spirit of the clause. I am of opinion that Abraham Lincoln *is* the President of these United States, bound by the duties of his office, and entitled to all that respect which the laws of God confer upon the civil ruler. Dr. Hodge, of Princeton, in a recent article on the war, remarks: "That the government to which our allegiance is due is the National Government at Washington, of which Abraham Lincoln is the constitutional head." The Administration is now the Executive Government, and will be during the period of its constitutional service. There is no other; and you can have no other without a revolution. This Administration, for at least two years to come, must conduct this war; and during this period the salvation of the nation will be in its hands. If this rebellion is to be crushed by force, please to remember that this can only be done through the constituted authorities at Washington.

By *supporting* this Government, I do not mean that the people should surrender the right of private judgment, or decline in a proper way to express their opinions of its policy. But I do mean that the people should so exercise this right as not to *abuse* it, and bring themselves into conflict with the duties they owe to the national authority. They ought not to slander their own Government. They ought not to speak disrespectfully of their civil rulers. They ought to sustain the financial credit of the nation. They ought to obey the laws, and sustain those who are engaged in their execution. They ought cheerfully to bear the burdens which are imposed upon them. In the time of war, especially such a war as the present, they ought to adjourn all minor questions, to frown upon all factious opposition, to lay aside the collisions of party strife, and unite as one man in supporting the national authority. They surely ought not to cripple and break down the very authority which is their only defense and safety, at the very moment in which the enemy is upon them. The Government should be wise; it should be efficient; it should remember that the people are thinkers; but when the Government, in such a crisis, taking counsel of its own wisdom, and all the wisdom it can bring to its aid, has enacted its laws and fixed its policy, then the people must sustain it, or civil society is a failure. I know that there are extreme cases of conscience, and enormous oppressions justifying a popular revolution, that qualify these statements; but no man of candor will pretend that in the loyal States we have reached any such extremities. Parties are quite apt to see such extremities where they do not exist; traitors always see them; yet I think this is a time when the people should not allow either politicians or traitors to spread confusion and discord in their own ranks.

I have thus stated as clearly as I can what I mean by the Government, and also what I mean by supporting it. The Government intends to prosecute this war to final victory; such is its public declaration to the world; and I ask you to give it your earnest and hearty support for the following reasons:

THE FIRST IS THE FACT THAT IT IS A GOVERNMENT, NOT ONE SO "CALLED," BUT ONE IN FACT AS WELL AS RIGHT. Allegiance of both sentiment and practice to government is a *religious* obligation. The Bible makes it such. "Government is a divine institution." Obedience to the powers that be is a moral duty. Disloyalty is both a crime against the State and a sin against the God of Heaven. Traitors, whether Northern or Southern, pro-slavery or anti-slavery, Democratic or Republican, editorial or political, traitors in public or private life, are sinners against God; they break the law of Heaven; and those who countenance or aid them, designing to do so, are partakers with them in this guilt. Have we a Government in this time of war—a legislative, executive, and judicial authority still existing in this nation? We certainly have; the action of this authority, moreover, is the supreme law of the land, and by the laws of God we are required to obey it. There is not a man in this whole land, whose property or services the Government may not command for the purpose of conducting this war. Some people talk about resistance, if this or that measure should be adopted, if conscription should be resorted to as the means of filling up the ranks of the army. Let me tell you that this means anarchy, and that anarchy means perdition. Let there be an anti-war party in the loyal States, forcibly resisting the national authority, or undertaking to do any thing of a compulsory nature in opposition to that authority, and you will have two civil wars instead of one. The national authority is the interpreter of its own rights and duties, as it must be if it be the supreme Government of the land; and no action of individuals, no resolutions of State Legislatures, no Conventions of Commissioners, must forcibly cross its path. You may at the proper time change the *persons* who wield this authority; but you must not touch the authority itself. This is sacred by the laws of God. To this, you and I, and all the people, owe the duty of loyalty; and by this I mean "the allegiance and service which the law requires of a citizen to his country, or of a subject to his sovereign." I have always been a law and order man. I am so to-day. For this reason I denounce treason as an atrocious crime. I believe it to be such. I can have no sympathy with men who make light of the sanctity of law. My Bible teaches me that the civil ruler is the minister of God.

THE SECOND REASON WHICH I OFFER FOR SUPPORTING THE GOVERNMENT, CONSISTS IN THE FACT THAT THE NATION IS IN A STATE OF WAR. I do not now decide what kind of a war it is, or whether it be just or not. I simply declare it to be a state of war. We have armies in the field, that have gone forth at the call of the Government, to fight the battles of their country. They are facing the enemy, and the enemy facing them. They are to win victories or suffer defeats. Now, what will you do in such a state of things? Will you desert the Government and army of your country in the presence of an armed foe, break down the one and starve the other, and thus force a peace upon the nation that will be its disgrace, and perhaps its ruin? Will you be indifferent to a struggle in which your own country is involved? Are you going to act the part of traitors yourselves by giving aid and comfort to the enemy? Surely not. I think better of you. I think better of the people of the loyal States. There is a principle of patriotism involved, which must have influence with every noble and generous mind. It is for this reason that an anti-war party, that in the time of war seeks to embarrass and perplex the Government, when it comes to be fairly understood by the people, is quite sure to seal its own fate. The Hartford Convention was so regarded in the war of 1812, I think undeservedly, yet it was so regarded; and the very name has ever since been a stench in the nostrils of the nation. War is an hour of peril; it is an hour of trial and suffering; it is an hour when the powers of a nation are put to the test; it is an hour when the national honor and safety are at stake; and hence I insist that the state of war gives special emphasis to the doctrine of allegiance. This surely is not the time for the people to desert their own flag, and seek to embarrass the Government which affords them protection. Then, if ever, a man should stand up for his country, and give to its public authorities his earnest support. He may desire peace; he should do so; but until the Government can safely make a peace, patriotism requires him to sustain it in prosecuting the war. This is always the surest road to a safe peace. Peace purchased at the price of dishonor, especially the inglorious prostration and ruin of one's country, is always too dearly bought. It is a greater evil than war. "I am amazed," says General Rosecrans, in a recent letter to the Legislature of Ohio, "that any one could think of 'peace on any terms.' He who entertains the sentiment is fit only to be a slave. He who utters it at this time is moreover a traitor to his country, who deserves the scorn and contempt of all honorable men." These are earnest words. They come from one who has a right to speak to the people, and urge them to support the Government in this terrible contest. In times likes these every man ought to uphold the national authority. This is our only safety.

As a third reason for sustaining the Government, I name the object of this war. By *object*, I mean the declared purpose of the Government in its prosecution. Upon this question there ought to be no mistake in the public mind. There surely is no occasion for it, since this purpose has been proclaimed in the most distinct and complete manner. Both houses of Congress have said to the people and said to the world, that the sole and only object of the war is to suppress the rebellion and restore the Union. In his Inaugural Message the President declared that it would be his purpose to execute the laws, with paternal tenderness beseeching the Southern people to return to their allegiance. In his Messages to Congress the President has announced the same purpose. The diplomacy of the Government with foreign nations bears the same stamp. In his Proclamation of September last, the President declares "that hereafter, as heretofore, the war will be prosecuted for the object of practically restoring the constitutional relation between the United States and the people thereof, in such States as that relation is or may be disturbed." It is easy to say, for political and party purposes, that the war has become an Abolition war, a war to put down slavery, a war for the negro, and not for the Union; this is the current slang of many newspapers; yet, so far as the Government is concerned, there is not the first word of truth in the statement. The declared purposes of the Government prove it to be absolutely false. Those who make the statement have the means of knowing it to be false. The position at first taken by the Government, is the one maintained to-day. I can not tell what God means by this war, but I think that no reasonable and candid man can be in doubt as to the purpose of the Government. Those who misrepresent this purpose do not state the truth, and some of them are justly chargeable with a willful falsehood.

But has not the Government resorted to the principle of *emancipation* in application to rebels, as one of the measures of this war? It has done so, and on the same theory that it has raised an army and built a navy. It has done so for the purpose of breaking down the rebellion, and restoring the Union. This is the express and only doctrine of the President. You may think it unwise; you may doubt its constitutionality; as individuals, we are of course entitled to our own opinions; but let us not forget that the Constitution makes the President the judge on both points. His judgment is final; certainly so until some competent court shall pronounce it unconstitutional. "We had better leave military matters" and military necessities "in the hands of those to whom they belong." Above all, we had better not make our individual opinions, without the means of an enlarged judgment, the rule of either supporting or opposing the Government, in this dreadful struggle for national life. We had better not let our pro-slavery or our anti-slavery affinities, whether gratified or not, become the law of our allegiance or the measure of our devotion to the public authority, in this hour of peril. I for one do not like the prevalent idea of the recent speeches of Wendell Phillips. I am an anti-slavery man through and through; I want to see slavery removed from this land, and will do all that I can righteously do to secure this end. But I am for the Union, slavery or no slavery; and this I do not understand to be the position of Mr. Phillips. I hope that I do not misrepresent him. I think I do not. I want to add that I have as little sympathy with those men whose only god is slavery, who would rather see the Union perish than saved if slavery is to be touched, who shout abolition from sunrise to sunset, as if the word itself were the end of all argument, and who clamor against the Government and seek to weaken the confidence of the public in it, because it has adopted emancipation as a war measure. Who are these men, and what are their antecedents? Some of them are unmistakably in sympathy with the rebels; and some of them use language absolutely treasonable—language which, if they were at the South and applied the same to the rebel authorities at Richmond, would cost them their lives. Claiming the right of free speech, they most sadly *abuse* it to their country's peril. I am sorry to say such things; I do not charge them upon any one of my hearers; yet the hour has come for plain talking. There is no disguising the fact that we have traitors at the North—men who are heart and soul with the rebellion. The fact is so, and we may as well say it.

Has not the Government, by military arrests and confinement, interfered with the liberty of some of the people in the loyal States? It has done so; and perhaps in this it has made a mistake, and perhaps it has not. At any rate, the object was to prevent traitors from ruining the country. The thing was done when the land was heaving with the spirit of revolution, and the fate of the nation hanging upon a hair; and moreover, when it was done, public sentiment approved of it as a just and necessary measure to save the nation. Now I will suppose that the Government misjudged as to these military arrests, either as to the entire principle itself, or in some cases as to the persons arrested; and then I respectfully ask, are we going to be so foolish, so narrow-minded, so blind to our duties, and so insensible of our perils, as for this reason to decline giving to the Government our earnest support in the prosecution of this war for the conquest of the rebellion and the restoration of the Union? Are we going to divide and contend among ourselves, and thus destroy our own power, with the enemy before us and the life of the nation committed to our charge? Are we going to paralyze the energies of the Government, and practically desert the army in the field, while we stop to debate the undecided question whether the President has or has not the right to suspend the writ of *habeas corpus* in a time of rebellion? No, my hearers, I do not think we shall. I think the sober second thoughts of the American people, if not their first thoughts, will lead to better counsels.

I appeal to you as the lovers of the Union; such I believe you honestly to be; and if I had the ear of the nation, I would appeal to that; and I would say to every man who loves the Union, that the object of this war, as declared by the Government, is to save the Union, and for this reason I would ask every man to put his shoulder to the wheel, whatever may be his private opinions about this or that measure. This argument, I know, will find a response in all loyal hearts. I do not expect that it will have weight with those who are willing to make peace on any terms, even at the price of disunion.

I URGE YOU, IN THE FOURTH PLACE, TO SUPPORT THE GOVERNMENT, BECAUSE SUCCESS ON OUR PART IS OUR ONLY NATIONAL SALVATION. I have always believed that we *can* succeed. I believe so now. Give us time enough—the question of time is a large element in war; and we can certainly triumph in the end. We can solve the problems of finance and the problems of the battle-field, and at last exhaust the foe and bring him to terms. We have the power. All we want is the will and the endurance.

How shall we succeed? I need not tell you that it must be through the public authorities at Washington, and that these authorities are absolutely powerless unless sustained by the people. I need not tell you that we must conquer a peace, or surrender to the enemy. Peace on any other basis is now utterly out of the question. Successful war is now the only peacemaker. Anglo-Saxon blood is pitted against Anglo-Saxon blood, and one or the other party must at last yield. If we yield, the nation is lost. If we persevere, as we can, the rebellion is crushed, and the nation saved. There is before us no other way of salvation. We are absolutely shut up to successful war, or disunion. To make any terms with an armed rebellion till it either submits or achieves its own triumph, is positively fatal. Mr. Barnes well remarks: "God treats with men in rebellion only when they submit to authority and law; and a government that recognizes a conspiracy and a rebellion, and which treats with it as such, is already at an end." Those who want the Government to treat with the rebels, are very wide of the mark. In the first place, they will not treat with us on any basis but disunion; and in the second place, if they would, we can not treat with them till they lay down their arms. We must fight them, and that, too, successfully, or die. It is a question of life or death on their part, and equally so on our part.

What, then, will you do? Will you stand back and simply look on? Will you spend your breath in criticising the Government? Will you be mainly occupied in laying plans for the next Presidential election? Will you foster the spirit of faction? Will you plot in secret places to distract the public mind? Will you encourage the rebels to hold on in this struggle? Are you going to give countenance and comfort to those who are doing all that they can to weaken the energies of the Government? In such an hour, in such a crisis, is it possible that newspapers and politicians will "persist, at all hazards, in spreading discord, bitterness, and strife among the people and in the army"? Is it possible that the people themselves will consent to be made the victims of such an awful folly? Let the people take this course, and the nation is ruined. Our destruction is sure. Fate is then at our very doors; and unless we arouse ourselves, and correct so great a mistake, the angel of death will pierce the very soul of our national life. I can not think—no, I can not think, that the great body of the people in the loyal States can be persuaded to deliver themselves up to such evil counsels. They are patriots; they love their country; and they will fight for it to the very death. They will not, they can not, consent to the dismemberment of this nation; and since success in war is the only method of averting this result, they will fight it through to the end. The peace men on any terms, the anti-war men, those who would sell out their country, the sympathizers with rebellion, those who spend a large part of their time in croaking, those who vilify and slander the Government, will either change their position or lose all influence over the public mind. There is intelligence in this country; there is virtue here; and, as I believe, enough of both to save the nation, notwithstanding the clouds that now darken the sky. Let England or France forcibly intervene, and let the President call the nation to arms, and you would soon see of what stuff the American people are made. You would see an exhibition of the character that is in them, and which being in them, will, with the blessing of God, carry them victoriously through this struggle. They are bound to go through. They can not avoid it if they would, and they would not if they could. The necessity is upon them. And this is true, whether the Government at Washington be Republican or Democratic. No party can administer this Government, or terminate this war, against the overwhelming sentiment of the people, that the nation must and shall be preserved. We may be delayed by our divisions on minor questions; we may prolong the war; we may, by the contests of party, put our country to great trial and even jeopardy; but we shall come to this at last. This is the position of the Northern people; and they never will forsake it, because in the very nature of things they can not. On this point I advise you to be of good cheer, and look hopefully into the future. Stand by the Government of your country, which is now your only salvation; and all things will come out right.

As to the fanatics and political lunatics, who look at this war exclusively from the anti-slavery stand-point, you need not trouble yourselves. They are not the Government, and never will be.

As to Northern traitors, I advise you not to be deceived by their treachery, or frightened by their bluster. Some of them are bankrupt politicians; and some of them never knew what the word *honesty* means. Some of them shout liberty when they mean slavery. All of them are the enemies of their country. Their creed consists in opposing every thing done by the Government to conquer the rebellion. Do yourselves the justice to understand them, and them the justice to despise them, and then have the candor to tell them so. "Such persons," says Dr. Hodge, of Princeton, "should at least be marked and avoided. All political support or encouragement should be withheld from them." I think they will be marked. In the public esteem they will at last go to their own place, and then they will stay there. True men, honest men, real patriots, men that have not played into the hands of the rebels, men who have devoted themselves to the salvation of their country, are the men whom the people will delight to honor. They will have a place in history, while the traitors will either be forgotten or remembered only to be detested.

I ASK YOU, IN THE LAST PLACE, TO SUSTAIN THE GOVERNMENT IN THE PROSECUTION OF THIS WAR, AS A DUTY WHICH YOU OWE TO THE LOYAL PEOPLE OF THE SOUTHERN STATES. There are some loyal people in these States; and they have suffered, and are suffering, at the hands of the rebel authorities at Richmond, to an extent that is perfectly appalling. They have been driven from their homes. They have been persecuted. They have been imprisoned. They have been murdered by hundreds. They have been forced by thousands into the rebel army. They have been hunted in the mountains, and dragged from their hiding-places, and compelled to fight against the flag of their country. A more atrocious despotism than that which Jefferson Davis now wields against Union men in the South, never disgraced any age. It is unpitying and remorseless. It is no injustice to say that it is set on fire of hell. We had supposed, that, at least in this country, the age of martyrdom was passed; but it seems that we were mistaken. There have been martyrs at the South—men who by ruthless and wicked hands have gone up to glory and to God, guilty of no other crime than allegiance to the supreme Government of this land. When the inside history of this rebellion shall be fully written, as in due time it will be, the civilized world will see what slavery is, and how it is fatal alike to the liberties of the white man and the black. Read the recently published volume of the Rev. Mr. Aughey, a Southern minister, entitled *The Iron Furnace*, giving an account of the sufferings and outrages inflicted upon Union men in Northern Mississippi; and your spirits will burn with unwonted fires. Other equally credible witnesses have testified to similar facts in other parts of the South. In one of the prisons of North-Carolina, according to a statement recently made, there are between three and four hundred Southern men shut up, simply because they believe in the old flag. This is their only crime. East-Tennessee has been ravaged, and her faithful sons persecuted to death. She has implored the Federal troops to come to her help. A gentleman last week returned to this city from one of the prisons in Richmond, about one hundred feet in length and thirty-five feet in width, and containing in a single room some two hundred and thirty men, some of them Federal prisoners, and some of them Union Southern men. The prisoners are furnished with no beds or blankets, and live on a pint of soup salted with saltpetre and a small piece of bread, supplied twice a day. The prison is literally alive with vermin. Every man has to lie down among them, and to be almost eaten up by them. This gentleman upon whose authority I make these statements, narrates the case of a Baptist minister from East-Tennessee, sixty years of age, who has been in this prison for more than a year. He was suspected of not being in sympathy with the rebellion; and to test him he was required to take the oath of allegiance to the Confederate Government; and this he would not do, and because he would not, he was instantly arrested, and has ever since been incarcerated in Richmond. He states many other cases of a like nature. One man was dragged from his home in Virginia, without his coat on, without his boots on, without the permission to go into his own house and bid farewell to his family. Another, a comparatively young man, has been repeatedly visited by his brother, and urged to take the oath of allegiance. But he will not. He is determined to rot there rather than violate his conscience.

Such facts stir my blood. They arouse my indignation against this wicked rebellion, and against the men who are its leaders. I have no rose-water diction for such things. I pity these martyrs. I honor them. History will honor them. They are among the very truest men in this land. They know what the rebellion is; and this is the reason why they speak of it so strongly. Thinking of them and feeling for them, I see one reason why I should earnestly support the Government of the United States. I want to see that great Moloch of death crushed, which crushes them; and this, I know, can only be done by successful war conducted by the national authorities.

What say you, my friends, in regard to this point? Are we at the North, who have had no such bitter experience, the men to look on with indifference? Are we going to divide our strength in useless debate, when our friends and brethren bleeding at the South are beseeching heaven and earth that we should be united? Have we lost our souls, our reason, our moral natures, our patriotism, in one general wreck of all that makes a man, pitching and diving upon the angry seas of party politics, the sport of our own selfish passions, and that, too, when the groans and shrieks of suffering patriots are calling us to the rescue? Shame on the man! Eternal shame upon the man who in such a crisis is unfaithful to his country and to the Government which is its only protection! Who seeks not to strengthen, but to weaken the national arm! Whose policy, plans, and words palpably betray his sympathies with the rebellion! Who has no earnest words of cheer for the soldier! Who would demoralize the army, if he could! Who would destroy its confidence in the Government! Who riots in the divisions of public sentiment! Who makes it his business to sow discord! Who under the deceptive cry of *peace*, is ready to welcome the dishonor and even the death of the nation! That man is my enemy, and your enemy — the enemy of the country as truly as was Benedict Arnold. He is no patriot; and to denounce him as a traitor is simply to speak justly of him. It is a virtue to abhor him.

I am done, my brethren, with this subject for the present. I have spoken plainly, I trust not offensively to your ears. I bring no railing accusation against this congregation, or against any member of it. I am conscious of no unhallowed bitterness of spirit; yet I am entirely in earnest. It is no time for men or ministers to avoid responsibilities. I will not. I shall not ask the newspapers or the politicians what I may say in this place. The newspapers and the politicians, yea, this church that has so long honored me with its confidence, and every man in it, and myself into the bargain, are to me lighter than a feather, in comparison with the interests of this nation at the present moment. I would disown my father and my mother, yea, I would disown every being in this world, sooner than be untrue to the flag of my country in this hour of peril. I care not *who* administers the Government. I care not whether the Administration be Democratic or Republican. When the proper time comes for me to vote, I shall vote according to my best judgment, and you will do the same; but until that time I shall in this death-struggle support the present Government, and that, too, whether all its measures exactly suit my notions or not. I shall do so because it *is* the Government, the *only* Government through which this nation can now be saved. I do not find fault with friendly criticism of its measures for the purpose of making them better; I do not complain of the newspaper press for seeking to guide as well as reflect public sentiment; this is all right and proper, especially in a land like ours; but a malignant and concerted attack, with the plain intention of breaking down the Government, and undermining it in the confidence of the people,—misrepresenting its policy,—seizing upon every possible occasion to damage it,—loading it with opprobrious epithets,—speaking disrespectfully of our national rulers,—styling it "the Government, *as it is called*" —all this, let me tell you, is a very different thing, and springs from a very different motive. It is not according to the laws of human decency, or those of God at any time; and at such "a time as this," when our rulers need the utmost sympathy and support on the part of the people, when they are bearing as heavy burdens as ever rested on the shoulders of mortal men, when according to their best wisdom they are doing all that they can to conquer the rebellion and save the nation, at such a time it is positively wicked. This thing I mean to rebuke. It deserves rebuke. The country is agitated with it to its very serious danger. Its tendency is evil, and only evil, and that continually. Such agitators, if they do not actually mean treason, are nevertheless serving the cause of treason as effectually as if they meant it. Their course is positively infamous.

Before pausing I want to say a word in respect to those unprincipled factionists, who are seeking to create the impression that New-England is the responsible source of all our difficulties, and that if the Yankees of New-England—in the elegant diction of these gentlemen—were "left out in the cold," then the Middle and Western States might very easily patch up a compromise with *their* Southern brethren. I am glad they say it, since it is in their hearts to say it. Saying it shows the men, and equally what they mean. New-England, however, need not, I presume will not, trouble herself with their sneers. She needs not my defense. There she is on the page of history. You can read her. New-England is the land of the Puritans, of the men who brought the principles of civil liberty to this country. The movement which made us a free and independent people was born in New-England. The war of the Revolution received its largest support from New-England. Massachusetts contributed eighty-three thousand and ninety-two soldiers to the Revolutionary army, and the States of Delaware, Maryland, Virginia, North-Carolina, South-Carolina, and Georgia, all put together, contributed only seventy-one thousand one hundred and thirty, or eleven thousand nine hundred and sixty-two soldiers less than the single State of Massachusetts. Bunker Hill is in New-England. Concord and Lexington are there, and some other places known to fame. They have school-houses there and churches, and no slavery. In New-England they recognize the dignity of labor. They have free speech there. They keep the Sabbath there. I believe there are some colleges in New-England. If I mistake not, Daniel Webster hailed from New-England. In New-England the people read, and write, and think. They have, to a good degree, "sound political information," quite as good as that of those who never heard of Webster's Dictionary, and were never guilty of looking into a spelling-book. New-England repudiates secession, and means to fight treason to the death. New-England believes in the doctrine of Government. She believes that this nation *is* a nation, and not a rope of sand. A few of her sons and daughters are in the West, indeed quite a number of them; some of them have gone as far as Kansas, and others even to California. New-England ideas, like New-England shoes and New-England plows, are quite a common article in this country. I think they will remain so. Somehow ideas after all rule the world, and New-England is the land of ideas. "Leave New-England out in the cold!" I think you will be mistaken. Let me tell you that New-England means to stay in the Union; she belongs to it and it belongs to her; she means, too, that the Union shall be preserved; and when you attempt to put her out, you will hear the crack of her Springfield rifles and the thunder of her cannon in a way well calculated to instruct traitors and cowards. I am amazed and indignant at this graceless and wicked slang upon New-England. If there is any lower deep this side of the bottomless pit, to which mortal man can descend, then I frankly confess that I do not know what or where it is. No, my hearers, New-England will stand by the country, and the country will stand by New-England; in this struggle the East and the West will be a unit; and with the blessing of God the nation will be saved and traitors will be disappointed.

www.ingramcontent.com/pod-product-compliance
Lightning Source LLC
LaVergne TN
LVHW010833120826
845149LV00016B/1361
9781418190149